DEATH *and* MODERN KITCHENS

JEFFERY W. MCKELROY

authorHOUSE

AuthorHouse™
1663 Liberty Drive
Bloomington, IN 47403
www.authorhouse.com
Phone: 1 (800) 839-8640

Published by AuthorHouse   07/05/2016

ISBN: 978-1-5246-1700-4 (sc)
ISBN: 978-1-5246-1699-1 (e)

Library of Congress Control Number: 2016910811

FOREWORD

This book is a collection of stories and poems written over a ten year period in various places during various conditions, physical, mental, emotional, etc. I never set out to be a poet and in truth find most poetry about as hard to digest as a nickel. I have, although, always wanted to be a writer, even as a child. I think I was around ten years old when I started writing short stories. I was about fourteen when my English teacher told me I would never be a writer. Of course she was sleeping with a High School football player so that tells you what she knew. After high school I didn't write much. I was forced to join the Army by my desire to eat. It was the end of the 1st Gulf War. I left as soon as I could. I was a good soldier but it wasn't for me. I worked several jobs, radio DJ, prison guard, machine shop monkey, etc. For some reason I got married and joined the Coast Guard. I guess it was what I thought I was supposed to do. While I was stationed in Alaska I started writing again. It was 1997. I bought my first computer for $2,000.00. I was eventually assigned to the Coast Guard Cutter Dauntless in Galveston, Texas. My marriage fell apart and I found myself living in a loft apartment on the Strand with a towel, a plate, a fork and my computer. During this time I drank heavy, sailed around the Caribbean and wrote. I kept writing and two years after riding out hurricane Katrina in New Orleans I published my first book, American Ghost. Shortly after I moved to the west coast but during my time in California I also participated in the earthquake recovery efforts in Haiti and the oil spill cleanup after the BP Deep Water Horizon disaster. I never really intended to publish any of this. These poems and musings were for my personal enjoyment or were some sort of personal therapy. They were a chest of drawers where I tucked things away late at night. Some of these stories are personal accounts. Some are observances. Some of the characters are me, some are not. Some are just pictures painted with words. At any rate, in some way they all come from some sort of truth. At least that's the way I remember it.

Outside the window, neon lights that buzz above city streets,

Murmuring in the alley,

Some bum screams for "**Jennifer!**",

Rats scurry in subterranean layers, while tourists sip hot and sour soup in China Town dives.

Drug addicted, wannabe-pinup-queens shill their wares on stage at the Roaring 20's.... a dollar at a time.

Drunk salesmen talk about "the close!", pounding fists on tables,

Spilling their beer on their ties, cheap ties, cheap beer, matching combination.

My waitress's look of contempt draws me back in from my window gazing, reflection watching,

She hasn't washed her dreads.......... ever.

Gelled up faux-hawked, striped shirt wearers screw up the juke box, ask to put the game on, laugh too loud,

Time to leave.

The tiny dinosaur was once big.

He started out small.

We put him in water to make him grow,

and he did.

Later we took him out.

He got small again.

The tiny dinosaur sits in the window now,

Drying out, staying small,

Waiting for the water.

My clothes smell like train smoke and my fingers are yellow with nicotine. My mind is clouded with thoughts of a meal and a wash and a drink and a young girl all too willing to defile herself for me. I spent all night in some dirty used up country bar with all the dirty used up people that live there and die there and never were there. Now I have to pay for it or maybe I can just pass go and collect 200 dollars like I usually do.

Burnt face Jake says I'm not as much fun as I used to be and he tells me a story about me getting drunk and dancing the mambo on a pool table with a midget during Mardi Gras. It sounds funny but it wasn't me. I don't know who he's talking about. Burnt face Jake has been huffing gas all morning long and he smells like my '54 Chevy. I slept in that thing for six months when I first came here but they eventually towed it. I was going to get it running someday. Maybe I've run out of some days. Jake hasn't. He's got plenty left and he always tells me about 'em.

Helen slops the drinks now at the Abbey. Elisa left last year. She headed back to New Jersey with the tattoo artist that used to work on Canal. They said they were going to get clean when they got there. They just needed a change of scenery.

Maybe I need a change of scenery. Or maybe I just need another drink.

Twilight fades to dusk and dusk into night and a silver moon rises over this carnival to light the way for the freaks and geeks and pinheads that show up nightly to perform. Venetian blind shadows cast themselves on the old wooden floor of my room while beams of moonlight dance in the smoke rings that float up from the burning cigarette in the ashtray near my bottle of gin. It's hot in hear but not as hot as it is out there. I better let things cool off a while before I show my face again.

A rumbling builds across the river from the thunderheads that have been growing all day. The sound makes its way over the city and echoes off the buildings in the CBD and shakes the windows in the Quarter. Birds take flight and gypsy vagrants take shelter and sing their songs under tarpaulins in the alley. Billy puts down the tattoo gun and steps outside to take a break and watch the light show. Even I sit up in my bed and pull open the blinds to get a better look.

The rain comes down hard and sounds like someone is dumping out a bucket of nails on the tin roof of my apartment. The walls weep and the window seeps and it makes all the sadness in the world almost tangible.

"Take your medicine jackass.", I think to myself as I pour another glass. I've run out of limes and I've run out of soda, drinking it straight now.

I wonder if Sheila is working at the Three Legged Dog. I wonder if she's still talking to me. I wonder how Tim is doing. He had been making time with the spent piece of used jet trash that lives across the hall from him until he found her with someone else down at Ryan's Pub. Things didn't go too well and it all came to a head. I don't know the entire story but I do know that he busted in her door and pissed on her bed just before she got home. That's not normal.

The rain has started to slack up and the thunder seems to be growing more and more faint by the moment. My little fan does no good in this heat. I get up and open a window half expecting to trip over the cat and then I remember that she took him with her. Well, at least she left the booze. It's going to be another long night but at least I'm well prepared.

People when not appalling are funny.

Oklahoma people are even funnier.

I'm sitting at the bar of the Oklahoma City Airport.

No one knows how to order a drink,

Or pay a tab,

Or chat up a girl.

Black chicks always order wings,

Rednecks always order Bud minus,

I always order one more.

The light is fading from the sky and soon my flight will be here.

I want to be home but no matter which airport I am drinking in,

I will be missing someone.

She said,

"It stinks in here!!!"

No shit.

That's because I've been drinking and smoking all

night.

Outside,

Cottonwood drifts like snow on a sunshine breeze against an evergreen background.

Hurried cars wiz by on city streets,

Dodging pedestrians and cats and dogs.

Hippies are on the corner with their signs and their false sense of accomplishment.

Morning brings me nothing but a reaffirmation of the pin prick sadness that stabs at my heart.

The boring self-important losers that walk this city clutter up my view and taste like vinegar in my mouth.

I can't wait for night to fall and cloak it all in darkness, hiding us all from ourselves.

Spider

I let a spider in here

It was a small black spider

It was of no matter

It had no fangs to speak of

Too small

I didn't mind feeding the little bastard

Because he was of no concern

After a while he got bigger

He grew

His fangs got larger too

Before they had no bite

Now they do

Now in my room, late at night,

It is only me and the spider

He is huge and lurking

Waiting with his fangs drawn

He has always hated me

He has always wanted my death

I was just trying to feed a spider.

What to do?

I think I will kill him before he kills me.

Box Car Drinking
NEW ORLEANS, LA.

In a small town with a big sky I found an open road. I wanted to take Angie with me but she was too fucked up on this or that or maybe herself. I don't know.

I settled on riding in boxcars and feeding on trash.

A good night was a cheap bottle of wine and maybe some hobo hash.

Riding the rails was never easy but it was better than having a job.

Banjo pickin', late night drinkin'

Camp fire singin'

All things come around in turn.

I'll travel this road as long as will, will let me.

I was sipping wine from a plastic Mardi Gras cup while sitting on the
tailgate of a beat up '75 Ford that had seen better days.

The Spanish moss laden Oak tree a couple hundred years old provided
shelter from the sun and relief from the oppressive Louisiana heat.

My boots were all muddy, just like my shovel. The work I had done had proved
harder than I had anticipated. My shirt was soaked with sweat.

I didn't care though, I felt good to have it all behind me and I smiled
as I took a sip, thinking about good days to come.

After I had caught my breath and started to feel the wine a little I jumped down form my
perch. I grabbed the shovel and threw it in the back before slamming the tailgate shut.

I opened the driver's side door and picked up my dirty old cowboy hat and placed it on my
head. I moved back to the back of the truck taking a Chesterfield out of my pocket.

I lit my cigarette and stared at the little mound of dirt I was leaving beneath the oak tree. I smiled.

It's funny............ what it takes to get a woman to shut up sometimes.

1am

DENHAM SPRINGS, LA.

It's 1:15 in the am. I am sitting in my kitchen, drinking wine, smoking, thinking. She is asleep. The coolerator hums, slight buzz of a TV. in the back ground, something about politics. For me it's just this Formica table, pack of smokes, notebook and a pen.

There is a light over the stove and in this room all the trappings of a modern kitchen, microwave, self-cleaning oven, the whole thing.

It's cold outside.

Here in the dark amongst pots and pans and left over bacon grease I dream of a time when there was so much more than this.

There was a time when every road led to somewhere and every woman….. well.

Big time change, I never did.

I still want the same things… Life, love, a little adventure, something new once in a while.

I think I might take a drive in the morning, in a few hours.

I'll climb into that '54 Bel Air, pump the gas twice, turn the key, give it about 15 minutes and head down the road.

Maybe I'll get a new tattoo.

Maybe I'll just go to bed

These are the lean times, the bad times. There is no

inspiration, no interesting people or conversation or

artistic acts of passion and violence. Just me, just me

in the kitchen with half a bottle of merlot and a

macaroni dinosaur. The macaroni dinosaur and I are old

friends. He lives on the door of my coolerator in

ignorant bliss. He doesn't care if I stay up late, or

spill my drink or sing too load. He doesn't count how

many times I fill my glass.

The macaroni dinosaur is always around in all his green

construction paper glory, a little faded by time but

still my friend, still macaroni, still green.

Rainy Day in Miami

The rain won't stop coming down long enough for me to get another pack of smokes

The gin is soaking in

The thunder sounds like the Southern Pacific going by

Leonard Cohen is in my ear

Neon lights flicker in puddles on the street

The bums hustle for change

Taxi cabs, parking lot attendants, prostitutes, tourists...........

It's 80 degrees and my air conditioner doesn't work

Bell hop said he'll fix it

We'll see

I'm hungry but not enough for Cuban food.

I was ten. I stood in the rain waiting for him to bring the eggs out of the coop. I held the basket. He didn't understand why the rain bothered me. I didn't understand why he didn't understand. Nothing bothered him. He was smooth. He had been through it. That man made five invasions in World War Two, but all I knew was that he was my Grandfather. He was taken prisoner twice and always made it out. He saw so many things and loved us all. I didn't know that super heroes could die.

The smell is different today,

The air is different today.

In 1972 there were no ATMs and people stood in line at the bank in 3 button suits

Smoking cigarettes,

The ash trays were placed three feet apart along the roped off line and they were filled with blue

Aquarium rocks.

Cars sputtered along black top hard balls spitting out toxic gas but nobody seemed to mind,

We were poor and had to go to the washateria but mom always had money for Chocolate Soldiers.

The library was an outing, a doughnut a luxury.

I was so scared, I never knew where my next meal would come from.
I was so terrified that I would have no place to live.

Now it all seems so foreign. People squabble over stupid things… titles,
names, disinformation. "I'm a Democrat", "I'm a Republican".

You're a tool.

The Blue Jay outside knows nothing of this. He wouldn't care even if I explained it all.

Big time loosing,

Laying in my sick bed,

Cars pass by outside my window but it sounds like waves,

Crashing on the shore.

I wish it was, I wish they were.

I found my way home from the pub by pure luck,

Maybe it found me.

It's gotten too early too soon and golden morning light washes over everything

In here.

The cat yawns, the house creaks and I don't smell too good.

I guess I should get up, get a drink, something.

I feel like the cops are after me but I don't know why.

I hate this hippie town, this fake place with its losers, its shit talkers, its lack of art or anything interesting.

There's a hole in the boat and the Captain has the gout. There has to be some way that we can get out of this trouble we're in.

There's a mole in the den and the bell has a crack. Thunder is breaking over head and there are termites in the mast. The seas are angry and the waves are coming over the forecastle. Jimmy is looking through the bull nose to find our way home. The North Star is obscured by clouds and the white caps rage in the wind. Random creatures of the deep find their way on deck only to flop over the stanchions again.

We must rig up the tillers for the steering has gone out and we'll do it all by block and tackle.

The rain drives hard and coats are no good when God decides he's pissed.

Dirt Road

VICKSBURG, MS.

Dirt road

Trailer park

Phone booth

No phone

Howling dog

Milky moon

Crickets play fiddle

Shit! I dropped my fork.

Well, Doo-Doo-Water Jones and DJ D. Dribble used to hang out at the Lamp Lighter Lounge on Esplanade. The country was in a deep recession and this was about five to ten years before the urban revival of the 1980's. Needless to say New Orleans was a mean place to be in those days. They were a couple of street-toughs brought up hard in the projects near St. Louis number 1. They moved on from purse snatching and petty theft by the time they were in their early 20's. In these days they would get together at the lounge, drink "Shake'em Ups", smoke grass and think up new scams.

Doo-Doo-Water was always dressed like a gentleman, suit and tie, fedora, nice watch, DJ Dribble was more of a slouch clothed in cheap track suites, big jerry curl.

One night after drinking too much and smoking too much and thinking too much they decided to get some quick cash. Doo-Doo-Water had a two dollar pistol and a head full of rum. The DJ was high on smoke.

They left the lounge and walked over to Decatur. They found a little red haired girl talking on a pay phone outside of the Abbey. No one was around. They figured it was owed to them. "Give us your purse bitch or we kill you where you stand!", Doo-Doo shouted, holding his gun.

"You heard!' yelled Dribble as she dropped the receiver.

"Don't shoot!", She said calmly, as she reached into her purse, "Please, just take my wallet because it has all of my money in it but I need this other stuff."

"Whatever bitch, hand it over", said Doo-Doo.

And at that The red-haired girl dropped the purse drawing a loaded 38 revolver, leveled it at the two thugs and did Gods work. The blast from her hand cannon could be heard in Jackson Square. Pigeons took flight and tourists ducked for cover. It was the sound of thunder as she blasted away until the rounds were spent and the two toughs lay bleeding out on the cold ancient ground.

Good job Red.

Rain
NEW ORLEANS, LA.

It was moonlight and fog, the smell of lavender and cigarettes.

Box fan, naked light, cheap couch,

Cheap booze.

Sound of a river boat organ in the distance,

Night birds close,

You closer.

In the old house, in the golden evening light,

Dust dances, cats yawn, and I tell my stories to myself.

There is cotton in the field,

There is cattle in the barn, nothing needs tending.

I will drink deep tonight the swelling seas, the rising tide,

I will quell the storm,

I will wait.

And how is her sleep tonight?

Mine is not too good,

Staring at an American moon with Irish eyes,

Through a tobacco lens,

In a Guinness haze.

Want for different times,

Want for different days.

Tomorrow the plow,

The tax man,

The boss,

Tonight, the drink and the memory of the favor of a woman that can never be mine.

Decatur was always my friend, when no one else was. That street was my friend. Late night strolls near Esplanade, jazz from some top room, howl of a dog, smell of trash, the distant moan of a train on the run. On the run just like me, looking for something new but finding nothing but the same old swamp. How fast these days pass, these days of youth and drunkenness. How fast we age.

To sit like a seagull on trash on that bar stool in the Abbey, I long for it. To have it all back, the possibility of anything.

Now, out here on the fringe in the bastard regions, I hate all of this.

There is no moon that shines, no song that sings, birds do not fly,

But somewhere in New Orleans there is the tinkering of a piano that plays just for me.

Rain in the Quarter
NEW ORLEANS, LA.

The matchbox rooftops stay afloat like Haitian boats in an angry sea while all of heavens sadness pours out over all of this.

Passing trolley cars sound like church bells calling people to worship.

Seagulls and prostitutes find shelter in the shadows of ancient buildings.

Lawyers and bricklayers find solace in a drink.

The raven is silent, the rat is waiting.

I am writing it all down.

Flannigan's Pub
NEW ORLEANS, LA.

In evenings gathering gloom as twilight fades from the sky and the nights first stars shine through the firmament, night birds begin to sing their sad refrain while the rest of us settle into bars and cars and taxi cabs or lonely recliners in empty rooms to watch the evening news in the perpetual blue glow of a tv set. I found a spot at the bar at Flannigan's Pub and was content to watch fruit flies dance around to the tune of drunks smashing bottles outside while a distant riverboat played its organ. Like ants in amber the bar flies found a home in my pomade but it was of no concern. I would comb them out in the morning. I'm not ready to change my oil yet. It wasn't my fault, I lost my hat in an alley. That wasn't my fault either, I was hiding in the alley from the cops. To tell the truth, the whole thing wasn't my fault. You see the cops were chasing me because the bottle I had shoved in my pocket was sticking out but that had nothing to do with me because the man that sold me the pants had assured me that they had deep pockets. It's a long story and I just don't feel right telling it without my hat.

The truth is, that when the hours grow late and the color drains out of the world leaving us with only shades of grey, I find comfort in blue neon and nogahide, amongst bottle blondes past their prime and Friday night business men out on the prowl. I find comfort in swirling smoke and recycled jokes and the chance that Jim might give me one for free.. if I'm tipping…. and I've paid my tab.

The can is on random and it plays a really bad song that my father used to sing when I was a boy as we screamed down the highway in his '81 Buick Regal on our way to his next sales call. "If I had time in a bottle"….. I'd drink it.

I don't understand why anyone ever smoked Lucky Strikes, they burn my tongue but then again I drink High Life so who am I to judge?

Outside on the street, after a few drinks, the rattle and clang and grinding metal sound of the Southern Pacific in the distance echoes off ancient walls and sends cranes into flight, silencing night birds and disturbs bums in cardboard blankets. I think I'll go to Franks Corner, see if anyone has seen my hat……….

24

I took a walk along a railroad track, dropping bread crumbs so I could find my way back.
Storm clouds were rolling in from the west, I had a new fedora and two pocket vest......

With buttons down the front, and my steps were light for a man
wearing engineer boots, black hair grey roots.

A few stray rain drops stopped by for a visit knocking thirsty kudzu leaves around,
drawing steam up from iron tacks, seeping into creosote ties.... against grey skies.

Renegade white clouds against a pumpernickel back drop race
by in a hurry, guess they've got some place to be.

Not me. I got nowhere else to go, but down this railroad row.

There's a little white house growing in the weeds ahead. It raised a family
here along this river before the trains came when schooners brought supplies
from Vicksburg, time tried to take it but it demands to live instead.

The porch is gone and so are the kids but the bullet holes
are still in the walls, John is buried out back,

Betty left when they laid the track.

The fiddles don't play but the tall grass sways high on the embankment walls and I
kick rocks and flick off bugs as the storm crackles and clangs in the distant air.

Chinatown smells like cabbage and bad dreams, ducks hanging in windows. Strolling the streets, avoiding midgets hiding in alleyways, hands in pockets, loose change jingling, whistling past the grave yard. I was hiding under the stairs but time found me. It finds us all and collects it's fee….. a nickel at a time. It's funny, the things you remember when left alone with no one to take up your time or derail your train of thought. The paper boat I made after the summer rain as a child, my dog scratching my leg, the cake my mother made for me, Dad fucking the babysitter….. etc.

Trolley Bells and wayward seagulls, tourists from Oklahoma with gaping mouths and Eskimo Joe's t-shirts, cops and drug dealers, me and a martini. Jazz from a can is better than no jazz at all. This place is dead….. all the better. College students and wannabe socialites are "whooping" it up around the corner at the disco that just won't die. I'm listening to Bitches Brew, sipping vodka and olive juice, and not contracting Chlamydia.

I adjust my hat to scratch my head, I wonder what happened to all my hair. I pass that thought up like a sign on the highway, feel around, find my wallet…. good, it's still there. Why wouldn't it be? I don't know. "Can I get another?"

Outside it's dark, except for neon lights, and head lights and street lights. The sky is dark anyway, but the clouds are still there, you just can't see them, like me.

Small Dreams
GALVESTON, TX.

Big plans turn into small dreams as you gaze through the bottom of a half empty pint glass. Forgotten roads remembered, the touch of an old friend. Times change but we never do. As a child I remember riding in the back glass of my mother's Chevy. I remember everyone smoking in the bank, grocery store, airplane.......

I remember the lake, in the summer, late night, me and you, finding ourselves for the first time. 1985 Ford LTD, 8 track converter, getting the bras off was a little hard. I would have run away with you, maybe I did. I don't remember. It was too long ago, too far away.

My glass is empty, my cigarette burns my fingers.

The sun was beginning to light the sky as I shook off the frost of a chilly morning to step into the Clover Grill for a bite and a cup of coffee. The place was unusually bare and so I sat at a table near the window. On most occasions one dining alone is forced by the reputation of the place to sit at the bar where you are so close to the grill that if you incline too far over your plate you will come away without eyebrows. I watched the street through my own unkempt reflection in the window. Garbage men jogged behind the truck, yellow light flashing, dashing from one side of the street to the other on frosty pavement picking up fat bags of refuse to be tossed into the crusher. They worked in an artificial fog of diesel exhaust and frantic breath and were careful not to slip. The street sweeper followed behind, yellow light flashing.

I drew a little white packet of pure cane sugar from the little brown Bakelite container on the table. With index finger and thumb I smacked it against my other hand the required three times before tearing it open but not in two. I poured it into my coffee, and then the cream which I watched swirl around for a moment before stirring. I always enjoyed that brief moment of cream meeting coffee, the swirling of the thick white liquid dancing to the bottom of the cup and then spreading out. If you wait long enough there is no need to stir it with a spoon. The circulating of the hot coffee will do the job. It just takes patience. But a habit is a habit and I always stir it anyway.

The waiter takes his time taking my order and hums along to a Cher song the entire time before sashaying off to hand it over to the cook. I chuckle a little as I watch the heavily tattooed cook slap the meet patty on the dirty grill and cover it with a hub cap. The smell of cooking onions, burning bacon, meat patties, cigarettes........

Outside the firmament is turning orange. The cleanup crew has driven and jogged out of sight but I can hear them in the distance. The frost has melted turning brick streets wet. On wet pavement the tires of passing cars sound like the rustling of plastic bags. Bar-keeps open doors and hose off sidewalks while the delivery trucks begin to show up, loaded with beer, somewhere a jack hammer pounds at pavement.

A couple of night birds fly in to roost on the stools at the bar. In slurred speech they order chicken fried steak and potatoes and laugh about some private joke.

No one in a hurry ever comes into this joint. I'm glad I have nowhere to be. After a while I get my order and the check at the same time. My waiter forgets to refill my coffee, sashays off. I laugh a little. Outside my window a transvestite prostitute hobbles down the street with a broken high heeled shoe in one hand, a purse and a wig in the other. Her red sequined dress is stained and her fishnet hose are ripped. She stops at the corner to light a cigarette and flip me off for looking.

I finish my burger and try the fries but decide against them. I washed it all down with a little Old Charter from my flask. I push away from the table, stand up and step out and away, leave a tip, pay the bill, say "thanks", push open the door. The bell rings as the glass door closes and the brisk morning air burns my nose. I stand there in full sun watching my breath for a moment, remembering some faraway time………. but just for a moment. I straighten my fedora, and button my coat. I draw my shoulders in. I turn to go and I shuffle and shake down the street.

Drinking on the Levee
NEW ORLEANS, LA.

Trolley bells and seagull cries fill the air along the waterfront. The West bank is visible through the haze of riverboat exhaust. Cars crossing the bridge to there and back from there glisten in the sun like a sequined prom dress. The laughter of children the sound of a saxophone, the tapping of shoes, the booming base of car stereo, all sort of blend into a strange French Quarter static. I've been sitting on a park bench drinking red wine and eating a chunk of cheese that I got for free at the deli. It feels good to be alone, away from people, who are mostly fake anyway. No one leaves the house without a costume, without rehearsing their lines in the mirror, practicing facial expressions.

A stray dog finds me sitting there and stops for a moment. Even he is fake. He sits with his back to me but every time my cheese hand moves he turns his head, realizes what he just did, turns back around, waits again. I'd give him a little but he would just want more, maybe follow me, faking affection just to get more free cheese, like a woman.

Evening comes soon enough and lovers gather to watch the sun set behind cypress trees and the dark silhouettes of passing tow boaters and tugs. I take my last swig and stand tossing the empty green bottle into the trash can startling a few feeding birds gathered on the grass. With hand on hip I straighten my back and shuffle down from the levee to the street where neon lights beckon.

Star

TUCUMCARI, NM.

Dreams are like train smoke. Memories are like a woman, you can never force them. They come around when they want to. They flow like gin into a glass and swirl around in an intoxicating dance before they settle and are ready to drink. I rode in here on the rails with a dog named Star in a box car that had nothing more in it than a few rats and a blanket and an old can of tuna left behind by some bum like me. The life that I left behind was never a life of my own and the wrong that I had done never compared to all those that I had known.

Sure I tried the straight-way but always came up jokers. Now I'm on my own and I always come up aces. Big T.V., nice car, big house….. fuck that! It's a trap. I'll spend my life on the rails with a banjo and a can of beans and a dog named Star!

I stopped in a diner in Logan, New Mexico. I met a girl named Jill. She gave me a cup of coffee there. I liked her smile and the way she wore her hair. She reminded me of a warm summer day and how I always said I wanted a girl with freckles on her shoulders. Now I just want sleep and another can of beans.

Well, under this big sky is the kind of freedom that comes without caring and under this big blanket comes the kind of comfort without consequence. I would love if I could but I would have to be loved first. I guess Star feels the same way….. because he ate my can of beans. That's why I don't like dogs.

Some people that live in the Quarter float in like drift wood in a storm. It becomes one big log jam of human detritus and with the exception of a small few there is no escape. We all ended up here the same way. We were all a drift at sea. We wear our tattoos like scars from some forgotten war.

It was four in the morning on Decatur Street. I had spent the night slinging back Singapore Slings with some one-eyed ass whole with too many stories to tell. I finally had enough, left a tip, waved good bye and staggered through the plastic flap of the Abbey. Out on the street I was greeted by howling dogs and a train whistle and night birds. I spilled the contents of my stomach on the pavement just a few feet from the door.

In the aftermath and the fading gloom I made my way to the river. I found a spot on the levy next to a sleeping dog and his owner. She woke up with a half a bottle of Wild Irish Rose and was happy to exchange it for the company. I was happy to accept. We sat together in the morning light, sharing a drink, watching the boats go by as the calliope played and we scratched old Roy's head until we all fell asleep in the afternoon sun.

Looking back at it all now is like looking through a dirty glass of whiskey in a dimly lit bar but on the occasional day all becomes clear and I can see the events of that time as though they just happened. It was a perfect time, a convergence of planets, an alignment of stars. It was not a time to know but only to live. You had to be there.

I was on the wrong end of a marriage that had long lost its will to fight and I was doing all that I could to hold on for the sake of my religion and my three year old son.

Tim was an artist who had fought off a five year habit in New Orleans and come back to Galveston to try his hand at making it all right.

Danny had it good at home but wanted to do more but found himself doing more than he ever knew he did.

Tesa was a bright shining light surrounded by assholes who tried to keep her hidden. In the end she finished what Danny started. They saved me.

Before the story ended we lost a few friends along the way. Cancer got Pete at the age of 26 and Kate got herself way too early and for what reason she never let on.

It was a typical night in Galveston, sweltering heat, humidity you could drown in, but we were safe inside Molly's pub. We had been shooting darts and telling stories, some of them loud, some of them low. There were lots of laughs and the occasional tear when the Chieftains would play on the can. There were the usual drunks that night who wanted to fight but we never did. But this night there were six Chicanos from Houston who had been trying to start a fight all night. We had been successful at avoiding them all through the evening but as last call was called and we were pushed through the doors we had no choice but to move to the street.

We stood outside in our rolled up jeans and our greasy hair and laughed and joked and said good night to our lady friends as we finished our last couple of beers. As our friend Meg walked through the gauntlet of the Chicanos they began to yell out comments that would stir the heart of any respectable man to anger. At that moment I said "Hey, she's a friend of ours!"

That was all it took. They really showed what men they were when the six of them attacked Danny and me for nothing more than defending a woman.

The six of them jumped on us like wild cats but got more than they expected. We fought like bears, tearing and scratching, picking up everything in sight to use as a weapon. During the fight one of the interlopers hit his own girl and knocked her to the ground. Danny immediately stopped fighting to help her up but they kept punching him in the head.

Meanwhile I was pinned in a doorway by three of these bastards fighting for my life. It was just then that out of nowhere about five people came out of the bar to our rescue. Heads were smashed into parking meters, knives were pulled, bones were broken. Our beer drinking friend Alex shouted for us to hall ass, and we did.

Tesa picked up my hat and glasses and when we got home wiped the blood from our faces.

Afterwards we sat in our apartment licking our wounds, drinking Pabst and laughing our asses off. I miss those days.

Moving Sale this Saturday!

DENHAM SPRINGS, LA

This is the perfect moving sale for all you freaks! As some of you know I am leaving Louisiana and heading to California at the end of the month. So, everything must go! Sale items include:

- Statue of monkey wearing a fez

- Giant Chinese parade dragon head

- Giant wing from a Mardi Gras float

- Lava lamp

- Old ass computer that still works

- Hand carved African masks

- Aztec statue with a curse on it.

- Bronze crucifix found in the flood waters of Katrina

- Assorted household items and appliances

- Weird books

- VCR tapes

- Strange artifacts from around the world

And last but not least naked pictures of my ex-wife(this is perfect for you sick bastards that like big fat ass bitches that look like Jaba the Hut and smell like goat cheese)

So come on down to 113 N. College W. Denham Springs, LA. And buy some shit you don't need!

Drinking Makes You Think Funny Things

SAN FRANCISCO, CA.

I stood in the museum this morning, drunk as usual, looking at a painting of barren trees in winter.

It forced me to remember something I can't quite recall, a memory of disaffected youth that just barely slips from my grasp and is lost beneath the ice.

Alone in this painting under trees that offer no shelter from the sky, standing in snow and silence, mourning something I never knew.

Sad songs on a drunken piano on the wrong end of town. It's been a cool day with no jacket and the rain is still coming down. It pours off the roof tops and chases the cats from the street and we're all sitting in the black smith shop waiting for Lafitte. And it's one more round for Rosie, and Jim's had enough. Tim needs a cab and I could use a lime. It got late too early and we spent all we made but we'll sleep through tomorrow and do it all again.

St Philip and Bourbon, horses and carts, Monica and tourists, and the things you don't see. I'll stumble home tonight and wish you were with me.

He wished he had socks, standing there in the cold,

Tin roof having at him,

Sliding down,

Wishing he were me.

Well I always do what I can even when I can't. Sometimes it's a bottle of booze sometimes a bottle of pills. The clock ticks out with hours turning to days behind the great curtain that hides me from the world and wraps my room in shades of gray. Horse hooves clack on brick streets four floors down and roaches scurry across my hard wood floor. I just lay here in bed grasping this half empty bottle of warm red wine lost in thought, monitoring how I feel. With every sip it gets a little better and I think I might be able to go out and find something to eat today.

The light is fading and the rain begins just as my shakes stop. I throw off the ugly green blanket that covered my corpse and swing my legs out and put my feet on the floor. I knock over a few beer bottles on the night stand as I set down my wine. With all the effort of erecting a circus tent I rise from my grave, my floor is so dirty it feels like I'm walking on gravel. The whole place smells like a wet cigar.

I shuffle to the bathroom, kicking over beer bottles and whiskey bottles and various boxes along the way. A warm shower sounds good but I didn't pay the gas bill. It's a cold bath and a cold shave for me.

I found a suit that didn't smell too bad so I put it on. I can't find my hat. Where the fuck is my hat? I hope I didn't leave it in the burlesque club the other night. What night was that? My head was spinning when I hit the street and I stepped in every puddle as I staggered along the way to my hole. I fell down in Pirates Alley and then got up and pissed on the gate behind the church. I'm pretty sure I had it then. Oh! I know.

I go to the kitchen and there it is. I took it off and set it on top of the coolerator as I searched for a drink. Now I've got it. Now I can go.

I reach under the bed for my shoe box and take out a few bills. I don't know how long I'll be gone so I make sure I've got enough. I fold them up, I put a few inn my shoe, some in my jacket, a couple in my pocket and none in my wallet. I'm not new around here.

After a few more swigs of warm red wine I turn the locks and the knob and open the door to the tomb. I've got my hat and my coat and my shoes are tied tight. It's out the door and down the stairs and out into the street. It's hot today, even with the rain. Time for a chicken fried steak, maybe a glass of scotch, maybe a red head too. Who knows, I'll probably just end up on the floor again.

Drinking With My Hat
NEW ORLEANS, LA.

Fireflies in cypress trees and the darkness makes shapes as the last fire, orange light of day sinks into the swamp to smolder on the water. Alone now, just me and the bugs and a half empty bottle of booze that will be a full bottle of the shakes in the morning. The breeze brings the smell of food in through my window but there's no food on my table, just an ash tray half full of broken promises to myself. The slow sober sounds of a horn bleeding out from a scratchy old record keep me awake to make another preparation. I'm too drunk to mix it; I'll just drink it straight. My glass is so much bigger than the bottle but my aim is not good still. Spilled a little.

Mrs. Arceneaux
Baton Rouge, La.

It was November 1st, 1985 and Mrs. Arceneaux was in the bar again and everyone loved to see her. She kept a little one bedroom place around the corner just off Main but most nights she could be found sitting at the end of the bar sipping gin and tonic and talking about the old days, some good, some bad. She was born in 1920 and although times were tough growing up in Baton Rouge in those days, things were easy for a good-looking girl like her. She never had to pay for a drink or pay a cover or pay much attention. She had plenty of male friends content to do all of that for her. Although she had no need to settle down she did in 1945. Things were o.k. for a while; little blue house, white picket fence, the whole bit. Her husband was a member of the local Irish social club and liked to go out drinking with the boys and sometimes come home and slap her around a little. She finally got tired of it and moved out. Her husband turned up dead a few days later. Seems he got drunk and drown in the bath tub. People had their suspicions. By 1980 she was living in the fore mentioned one bedroom place with her boyfriend Stan and a couple of German Shepherds (Barney and Leo). She and Stan had both had their wild years but were both starting to get up there in years and they liked each other good enough so they decided to strike out together. It was rocky from the start. They both liked to drink all night and some say Stan couldn't keep up with the old lady's sexual appetite and this led to midnight fights and chairs through windows and cops being called. One day they found Stan in the pool, face down. People had their suspicions. Now Mrs. Arceneaux was alone, just her and her dogs and time to kill. She killed it at the bar with red painted lips and long gray hair that hung passed her hips. She liked to flirt and pass a joke and put quarters in the jukebox and dance by herself. That November night she said good by and walked home. A few days passed and she didn't come back and those few days turned into a few months. Finally the owner of the bar went to check on the old woman. He knocked on her door but there was no reply but he could hear the dogs barking, so he asked around. No one had seen her. Out of concern he called the cops and they came as slowly as possible. Having been unable to raise the tenant they obtained a key from the manager. Upon entering the home of Mrs. Arceneaux they found a disturbing sight, a grizzly scene plucked from the pages of Fangoria magazine. Human bones and teeth and hair were strewn about the apartment having obviously been picked clean by the two dogs locked inside. On the kitchen table a note was found. Mrs. Arceneaux couldn't take it anymore. She had seen all to be seen. It was a bottle of pills for her and her only concern was that someone please feed her poor dogs. Little did she know, she would be doing that.

Martini Time in Galveston
GALVESTON, TX.

It's four in the morning and Louis Armstrong is on the stereo and some guy that looks like Tom Waits is in my kitchen and Pete is smoking cigarettes on my big red velvet couch and I'm making out with a tattooed lady in the back. The whole place is filled with smoke and jokes and half-empty martini glasses. The trolley sings it's song as it goes by and some guy down stairs is trying to resurrect Thelonious Monk. The rain keeps coming down and so do we. Safe inside. Our little world that time forgot. Pomade and roses and big buffonts. I wouldn't have it any other way. Hey! Turn up that Thelonious Monk!

I woke up in St. Louis Cemetery sometime just after dawn. The night had, had its way with me and left me for dead with all the human detritus of the city's past. Morning comes down hard on a man who's full of wine and bad intent. My head was ringing like a church bell and sea monkeys danced in my corneas. The smell of wet earth and oak trees smelled better than my apartment but I wished I was there. I sat up with my back against the wall of a tomb and searched through my pockets for my cigarettes and my lighter. I found my lighter but the flint was spent and the pack of smokes was crumpled and useless like me.

Unsteady and weak kneed I stood up with the help of an iron fence around a grave and dusted myself off while scanning the scene of the crime for my hat. The sun was unrelenting even at this early hour and I could smell my pomade beginning to melt. I wondered what had happened to my hat. Had it been stolen perhaps? Who would want it? I think the damn thing is disgusting and I'm the one who got it that way. Just then a few feet away I spotted it. It was placed neatly atop the head of a perpetually praying angle. I retrieved the formerly lost article and returned it to its natural place of residence. Shaky and unsure I shuffled toward the street.

As I moved along the shaded lanes of the Garden District making my way to St. Charles I pondered my situation and made a vain attempt to recall the events off the night before but the only thing I could be sure of was that I had been drinking but that's a given. Now with pounding head and racing heart and sweaty brow I was sure that I needed to stop. I was a waste. I did not deserve my own breath. I had thrown my youth away on selfishness, drunkenness and vice. For the last twenty years I've prowled around in bars getting pissed and chasing skirts and carrying on with the dregs of the gutter. Maybe there is a chance for redemption. Maybe there is room at the alter for one more wayward miscreant seeking shelter from the storm that he himself called down on his own life. Maybe.

Tears welled up in my eyes as I reached St. Charles thinking of a life redeemed. I was still unsteady as I entered McGee's Tavern and sat down at the bar. Jill came over noticed my condition and with great concern asked me what I needed. "Just some scotch, whatever you have in the well. I don't care." Man she's got a great ass.

St John's Bridge

NEW ORLEANS, LA.

Well, I got a pocket full of graveyard dirt and a dead cat in a sack and I'm making my way to St. John's Bridge to get that bitch off my back.

I toiled all day with the trouble she brought and I knew there was one way out.

We got some HooDoo down here that can stop a train and fierce fire that will bring the rain.

Under the old oak at night in the fire's glow, in soft falling rain we meet and we speak in low growling tones,

and we know what we do and it's good even if it ain't, and we sing in the fire light and we pray in an alcohol haze and no chicken is safe.

We'll stop this evil and we'll bring our own torment and we'll raise Marie from her grave and you will do wise to watch yourself when the fires are lit on St. John's Bridge tonight.

Phone Call

KODIAK, AK.

Well, hello baby. I didn't think you would pick up, since it's four in the morning and all.

I was just sitting around drinking and thinking about how things used to be and wondering what you've been up too.

Oh, me? Great! It's been good. I have a lot of things going on and some really good friends out here. Yeah, it's great.

Hey do you remember that one time we did that thing in that place with those people we knew? Yeah, that was great.

Hold on. I lit my cigarette backwards. Ok, I just tore off the filter, it's ok, I got it.

So…. how have you been, how's life, you know?

Yeah, I was just sitting around having a beer, thinking about old times, wondering how you are. I've been practicing my guitar a lot lately. I know you used to hate it when I would play but I'm getting good. You wanna hear?

No? Yeah, your right it won't sound right over the phone anyway. Besides I've been drinking. That's why I called. I just wanted to see how you are these days.

Hey, do you ever talk to Joe anymore. Yeah, me neither.

You sound pretty tired. Yeah, me too but I've been drinking for a while. You know?

I found this picture the other day…… oh yeah ok. I understand. I was just up drinking by myself and wanted to call and see how you have been doing.

It was great to talk to you. Maybe I can fly out there sometime. It would be fun. Ok, yeah we'll talk about it later. I gotta get another beer anyway.

Alright I'll ca……. hello….. hello…..

The bitch hung up!

Unicyclists and Negro children tap dancing for dollars, hookers and hustlers and the unwary visitors who step in the road apples not caught by the bags that hang below the carriage horses ass. Around the corner is a corner café and I make my way slowly through the crowd. Like a drunken dance I move through the people, twisting and turning so as not to have to slow down or stop or touch anyone. An older couple on the corner wearing matching Hawaiian shirts have stopped to flip up their clip on sunglasses and check their map. A younger hustler on the other corner has stopped to put on his sunglasses and check out the older couple. A cop across the street has stopped to look at all of them. I reach the café unscathed, no one accosted me for directions or touched me either. No good looking waitress in this dinghy hole. All I get is a short, overly hairy gay man that makes a point of telling everyone he's gay at every opportunity as though no one could see it as soon as he stepped off the trolley. I mean don't get me wrong, I don't care that he's gay, calm down, calm down. It's the fact that he's short, hairy, and really gay that gets under my skin. But he's a nice guy and he gets me my coffee as soon as I come in. I never have to wait and if my eggs aren't the way I like them he'll fix'em right up. That's all I want anyway. A couple of eggs a cup of coffee and as little conversation as possible. Unless you're a young lady with a great set of tits and a nice smile, then you can talk my fucking ear off. I always have time to pretend to listen. I did meet a girl in here once and much to my regret it ended up exactly the way I wanted it to. I mean hell, it was four in the morning and the only thing on the streets were roving gangs of transvestite hookers wrapped in a cocaine fog that did not mask their violent intents. Best to take shelter in a brightly lit dinner than brave a sea of certain uncertainty. She had an ass like a loupgarou but her malefic muff was moist and I'm not the kind of guy that shows the dog the leash and then doesn't take him for a walk. It was all my fault. I sat at the bar to get a better look at her through my squinty beer clouded eyes. She was the type that's only my type at four in the morning and she seemed interested in me and that was enough, I had to act. Of course I invited her home with a sly drunken grin and she said yes as she wiped gravy from my chin. Her shift ended at six so there was a bit of a wait but by that time the transvestite gangs were gone and the sun was on the rise. We walked arm in arm down the old streets to my apartment a few blocks away. As the darkness continued its retreat and color began to seep back into the world and the poison worked its way out of my veins I could see that this was not the type of girl I would prefer to go home with. All of my friends are bums and still I was looking ahead and behind to insure the discreteness of the affair. The course had been plotted the bombs in their bays, it was time to be a man and do what I came to do. Oh Melpomene! Will you not have mercy on this poor slovenly-disenfranchised miscreant?! I was drunk and alone and the devil took his chance to deceive me. Now as we climbed the stairs to my loft my only thought was that I must just get through it. Here I stand before this double chunk, cream filled, sugar coated parvenu waiting to be devoured and it's all my fault. I did this. At least she was gone when I regained consciousness sometime in the late afternoon. It was straight to the shower for me.

Two eggs over medium and two slices of bacon, a little salt and pepper on the eggs. Thank you sir. I've seen people eat ketchup on eggs but I still don't believe it.

Jimmy Said
New Orleans, La.

Well Jimmy said it was time to go as the piano music bled out from an old drunk's fingers and we stepped out of Lafitte's to drink malt liquor on the side of the A &P while an out of work trumpet player wailed for dollars and change to be thrown into his box. And it was too late for the calliope and it was too late for the drag queens on this part of Royal but we were all doing what we could and maybe the rain would come and maybe it would hold off and maybe I would drink another beer and maybe just pass out in the alley.

I walked for a ways, all the way to St. Charles and then to Race and Magazine. I found an unlocked door at the old orphanage and crept inside. No one was around so I slept in the day room and dreamt of a warm bed and big tits and a glass of scotch.

Like moths to a porch lite we found our way to our bar stools. I watched her dance from across the room as my friends ordered a round. She was a black rose, dark eyes behind dark clouds and olive skin and a scar and a heart

Disaffected, maladjustment

Tiki torches and cheesy Christmas lights and I would never drink here anyway.

She made her way over and we talked about nothing. I did a lot of nodding and she did a lot of smiling.

We fought a war against our better judgment and won.

She kept her boots on when we screwed.

She lived in a trailer under the overpass.

Now she lives in my head.

It's the only place I'll ever see her again,

She's a ghost.

Lost Dog
LAFAYETTE, LA.

September and loss,

Hopeless,

Sad,

Craving some kind of human touch,

Some kind of understanding,

Who? If not her then who?

My heart breaks.

I stood in a December rain as a child, a child of ten, crying, giving up because my dog was lost,

My father was a mean man and he yelled at me, "Stop It! Stop being a pussy, you fagot!"

That's how I feel

Alone in my feelings

You start to wonder if all women, all people are fake, yes, they are.

They all are, we all are.

My father said I was a fool, he told me to give up my vigil

I didn't

Christmas came and went and so did my prayers and for a time I thought God had abandoned me

He didn't

He was waiting

One night, a few nights after Christmas, there was a terrible rain (which is common in Louisiana in the winter) and through the thunder and the driving sounds of hard falling water I could hear a little yelp.

I thought it was imagined at first and I was hesitant to go to the door at first for fear of looking like a fool,

I went to the door and I opened it,

There in the driving cold December rain I found my poor little dog that I thought had been lost.

He was shaking and cold and so happy to see me

Me too

I cried

I loved that dog, I needed that dog,

I was ten years old and my father beat my ass every time he got a chance and my mother was out of her mind and me and that dog were a refuge for each other,

We loved each other.

That's how I feel now,

The part about him being lost I mean.

Sunrise found me standing on Decatur,

Alone and drunk, just the way I like it.

The whole city looked like a ghost town,

Just me and the pigeons and the cockroaches and the empty silence.

Aside from the birds and the bugs nothing moved,

Not the breeze, not a car, no people, no life.

I thought that this must be what Dresden was like after we fire bombed the place in the war,

Except most of our buildings and roads were still intact,

Just nowhere to live,

Well, the bars were still open and that was enough for me,

Flannigan's never closed, they rode out the storm,

I love the fearlessness of a drunk with nothing to loose.

I wonder where all the drag queens went for shelter, the transsexuals, the hustlers, the whores,

Houston maybe,

I can picture them in my mind leaving the city in a big caravan of depravity, running in their high heeled shoes, gold sequined purses in the air in one hand, the other holding on their wigs, screaming, falling down, ripping their fishnet pantyhose at the knee.

I laughed to myself and began to shuffle down the street to my car,

I was happy that everyone was gone, happy that the city had been flushed out like one big toilet,

I liked the silence in Jackson square, just me and Andrew and his horse,

Just us in our pulchritude.

I made it to my car, still unsteady from the deviance of the night, my breath like roses and sulfur,

Dropped my keys on the ground and I hit my head on the car door trying to pick them up and then fell back on my ass to sit Indian stile on the curb,

I laughed a little, then made another attempt,

With all the concentration of a safe cracker I finally made it in,

I climbed into the back seat where I wadded up my jacket for a pillow and stretched out to sleep it off,

Dry mouth, dizzy head, racing heart, racing thoughts…….. wish I could write this down…… wish I could….. wish

I waited until she laid her big fat head on her pillow and fell deep into sleep

I listened to Miles Davis in the kitchen

Drinking cheap beer

I crept over and peeked in to make sure she was asleep

I went back to the kitchen and opened a window

I climbed out slowly, wobbly, unsteady, laughing as I fell on my ass in the yard

I righted myself and opened the gate, looking like a burglar making his escape

I ran down the street with a prison break gait

I only had to go a block

I kicked open the door to the Hide Away like I owned the fucking place and life and laughter and everything she wasnt spilled out into the street and washed over me like a warm wave, like salvation, like comfort, like an old friend happy to see me

I strolled along the bar with a Miss America smile and a nod and a wave

I patted Jose on the back and shook hands with Frank and told Matilda that I like her hair (even though I knew it was a wig)

I had Joe set em up and I threw em back and I laughed and I sang Danny Boy over and over and over..

I drank with two Mexicans that just got out of jail, "me too!" I said with a laugh

I drank shots of Hot Damn, yuk! Somebody else paid for those.

I danced with a barfly to some Ella Fitzgerald song and pretended to enjoy it

I smoked a pack and a half

I stayed until last call and bid everyone farewell, Miss America smile, wave, nod, head for the door. Somehow I fell backwards through the door and landed outside flat on my back in the street with the two newly freed convicts helping me up.

I adjusted my heading and put my sheet to the wind,

Sailing back to port for the night.

I made my way through the gate, light and easy

I tiptoed through the yard

I opened the window and made my way in,

Mr. Davis had gone to bed so I had to be a little quieter

I eased in to bed, disgusted, unhappy, resentful, drunk, really drunk,

But happy about that, little victories.. still me.. still unconquered

Jenny
DENHAM SPRINGS, LA.

A silver moon hangs in a paper sky painted with water color red and blue and orange. Shadows grow long as the light fades from the world and drains all the color away to drape us all in shades of gray. Yellow light from a second story window of the little white house lights up a square on the lawn near the oak covered in spanish moss. Glenn Miller plays his horn through the time warp of a scratchy old record and fire flies flit around the old well near the tire swing. The river is still tonight but the frogs still sing and the beavers splash and the dragon flies buzz around the porch light while june bugs cling to the screen. And Jenny dances in the lamp light with a ribbon in her hair and the flowers that she picked on the bed side table and the sorrow in her heart. Her old cat just lays there in the chair waiting for bed. Jenny holds a picture tight against her chest and dreams of rainy days in Jackson Square feeding pigeons taking shelter from the rain beneath banana trees.

New Shipment of Polka Dot Luggage
NATCHEZ, MS.

"New shipment of Polka-dot luggage. Just in!", read the sign as I strolled by in a Raglan jacket with a 40s cut and a hole in the pocket. The cheap ass boxed wine I drank last night gave me diabetes breath and a headache to write home about. The night started off good. After I had a few swigs of Military Special rum I hit the street ready to slay the first baby lamb that crossed my path. I burst through the door and the street burst back like an episode of Gang Busters but without the AM hiss and atmospheric crackle. It was all police sirens and the slow hiss of passing cars on wet pavement and prostitutes cat calling from the Artists Café. I walked by the gutter punks and bums unaffected with purpose of movement and slight of hand.

Big plans turn into small dreams once you pass through the plastic flap of the Abbey. The smell of stale beer, rotten wood and some guy named Stan are always there to greet you. The old lady with the poodle sits in the corner as usual while the dog sleeps on the bar breathing in the nicotine air as it snores. Burnt Face Jake sips a suicide concoction from a paper cup in the yellow light of juke box that's playing the blues. My boots are wet and turn the sticky floor slick as I approach the bench to plead my case. New found glory greets me in the form of a cold Pabst. I drink as many down as I can while Joe Shit the Rag Man sits in a booth trying not to die. He'll make his way home soon. He'll walk down Decatur and cross Esplanade to make his way over to Frenchmen and finally down to St. Roch. Where from there? I don't know. It's all been flooded out and so has my engine.

I met a girl with tattooed flames on her arm. She had nice style and a pretty smile and she asked me back for a drink. Things got weird for a minute when we passed through the flap back into the world. I guess it was the realization that we were leaving together and we both knew what that meant. We strolled in the rain stopping to dance for minute to the tune of a river boat organ in a twirling alcohol haze near the old convent. I held her close and noticed that her hair smelled like wet flowers and tobacco. Her blonde locks were green in the light of the street lamp overhead. We looked at each other for a minute and laughed and then turned to go.

We climbed up the fire escape and climbed through a window. She had her key but she liked it better this way. A little one room place with a well-made mattress on the floor and no TV but a lot of paper backs and dime novels from a thrift store. I kicked over a bug bomb as I followed her in to the dimly lit kitchen to get a beer. It was High Life in can. We finished those and started on the boxed wine and laid in bed looking out the window and talking about how fucked up people are. She fell asleep with her head on my shoulder and I gently moved her off and slipped away to the only chair in the place. I sat there and smoked a cigarette and thought about how unfortunate it was that we got too drunk to consummate the friendship but it's probably for the best. I helped myself to a plastic Mardi Gras cup and a little more wine and I put my cigarette out in a crystal ashtray and then realized it was a candy bowl. Oh well, too late now.

I slipped out the front door and headed down the ancient stairs that lead to a hallway, that lead to a courtyard that lead to the exit. I stepped out onto the street again and shuffled home as the orange light of a new day began to push back the night just behind the rooftops of a sleeping city.

Rainy Day at the A&P

NEW ORLEANS, LA.

I bought a pack of parliament lights and stood in the doorway of the A&P until the rain stopped. Covered carriages rolled by, pulled by mules in flowered hats. Somewhere a jazz band cranked out funeral music while pedestrians splashed through the streets sending the reflected colors of the neon signs in the puddles scattering. The sea monkeys in the potholes, fat with rain, sprang to life and began to dance. The pigeons came back. Fat drops fell from banana leaves and the smell of jasmine and trash floated in on a cool breeze. The moon came back out like a great big spotlight on all the bums and gypsy hacks and two-dollar whores at the Artists Cafe. Out there in the dark a dog howled in the alley and a cat sang back as the thunder rolled in the distance. I lit a smoke and rubbed my face and moved my fedora to scratch my head. I decided to walk a little before the rain started again. Maybe I could get some coffee and some toast at the diner or maybe just save the money and pick up a bottle of Boones.

Swagger

NEW ORLEANS, LA.

With two days off and pocket full of fresh bread I made my way down the down town streets with a swagger that would give any young girl heartburn. I kept my head covered with a new black porkpie hat with a feather in it. The grease in my hair adhered to the sweatband helping to keep it on in the stiff breeze blowing up around the bend of the river. My wallet chain clanked against parking meters and gutter punks on Decatur. My stomach growled as I passed Franks.

The sun was no friend of mine by the time I got to Frenchman but the shade of the buildings found me there once I crossed the street to get to Billy's shop. The bell rang as I stepped in. I checked in with the girl at the counter and flashed a smile and she gave me one back but Billy wasn't ready so I stepped back out and went next door to listen to a swampy jazz band with too much clarinet waist a little of their time on two old drunks arguing at the bar. They could tell I was interested and they seemed hopeful of maybe drawing a crowd but I was just there to pass the time with a cocktail while Billy finished his drawing. I had a few and figured it was enough so I went back to the shop and found Billy ready to go. He shaved my arm and applied the stencil and got to work in the usual fashion. In just a few hours it was done. I had a new deck of cards, a banner, the whole bit. It looked nice and I tipped him well.

By the time I left, the moon had chased the sun out of the sky and the city had taken on a different air. Most of the tourists had either gone home or were woohooing on Bourbon Street while the street hardened nighthawks swooped down to reclaim their nightly roosts. I stumbled in to Aunt Tikis with a day old shave and a new tattoo and settled down on a stool next to Horse Face Sally who was sipping a dry martini out of a plastic cup. I like it better this way, she said as she munched an olive with her mouth open. I just looked away. I gazed out the door and thought about the people on the street and the sticky bar and Amy and my new tattoo.

On a summer evening Danny and I were lurking in the shadows and shuffling down the streets of the seedier side of Tijuana, Mexico that is, when we were approached by a man of small stature but formidable size. He inquired as to the reason for our journey into the unsafe and foreign regions of the city and we informed our new fast friend that we were in search of something, shall we say, illicit. He scratched his chin and looked around as if to make sure that the coast was clear than motioned for us to follow him down a nearby alley. Past the prostitutes and junkies through puddles of piss and gasoline down a broken bricked street of a city with in a city we trekked through the alleyway. Up to this point in our visit we had purchased bottles of tequila nearly a foot tall for two dollars American and eaten like kings on another five but we were soon to realize that aside from a donkey show we hadn't seen nothin' yet.

We came upon a man with large U-haul box about waist high. In the box were cats of various sizes, colors and conditions. The man was happy to see us and motioned that we come closer. We negotiated a price and shook hands at five dollars American and everyone was pleased. The man with the box began to fish around in the box in a magnificent fashion as though he had learned his technique in the lounges of Vegas. In short order he produced a calico cat which he held suspended in the air by its tail. He smiled at us with his one gold tooth and his other one just yellow. We winced. He began to swing the cat in a circular motion in the most spectacular manor. Over and over again he swung the cat as it howled like a police siren as it came close, then far, then close again. Then without warning, at the top of the spin he released the cat launching it into the air. The cat flew into the sky, up through the clouds, into the ionosphere, through the hole in the ozone, past the moon and into time itself.

Then it began its decent. Slow at first then aided by gravity it picked up speed again passing the moon, back through the hole in the ozone, through the ionosphere and bam! Right back into the box. The two men stood there smiling and nodding their heads, very pleased with themselves. Danny and I stood there in awe. I'm sure that if you've ever been to Mexico you've seen a lot of things. But if you've never seen the Tijuana Cat Toss then my friend you've seen nothing.

Another cold front moves in over the warm waters of the Mississippi that spill out into the Gulf and the fog forms and pours into the Crescent City at night like the sacred moment when cream meets coffee, waiting for me to stir it up like the traffic on I-10 in the early hours, rushing in and dispersing throughout the old quarter, the business district, the West Bank, to the offices, the schools, the hotels and the business meetings. Everyone wakes up to stillness and peace and the sober somberness of a blurry world devoid of color and shape. Everyone lowers their voice a little and the song of the city takes on a funeral tone as if a ghost is moving through the streets visiting every house and asking every man to account for his life thus far. The anxiety is thick enough to touch, to feel, to dance with for a moment. People drink their coffee while they look out through the window waiting, watching as if for a spectral visitor. The shadows that have ruled the night are running from the rising sun looking for a place to hide, to wait it out. Best to draw the shades and drink that coffee alone.

I'll wait it out in this café by myself reading a book I have pulled off the shelf. It is a hip little place and these old crumbling books are just for show but I do this a lot and no one ever says a word to me about it. Besides, it saddens me to just let an old book by some obscure writer whose day has passed just sit in the dust and the humidity on a bookshelf until the spine falls off and the paper rots and termites eat their fill. These books contain the souls of these writers, these people, maybe all that is left, all that is remembered of people who were just like us, who walked and talked and sang and loved and fell down drunk and woke up the next morning with vomit on their favorite shirt and wondered why no one would return their calls. Maybe I'm just talking about myself here but it would be nice if someone was listening. It would be nice to know that 100 years from now someone will pick up my soul and thumb through the pages a while and look at what I loved and what I thought and maybe care some for me. That takes compassion. There isn't much left of that anymore. Compassion has become like an old hat that you like but it doesn't go with anything so you keep it in a box in the closet. Or maybe more like that old dog of yours. You had time to love him when you were a child but you're all grown up now and ain't got no time to play.

I thumbed through the soul of Mark Twain once in the form of the autobiography of Samuel Clemens, such a happy man to have had such a tragic life. Maybe it is redundant to say that life is tragic. It is tragic from the moment of birth and the tragedy never ceases. How is it possible to feel more love than in the womb? Surrounded by the one who gives you life, protected, fed, warm, no need or want for anything. Then suddenly, without cause or provocation, without the stain of sin or any kind of guilt you are spit forth in a series of horrendous pushes that leave no doubt in your mind that you have overstayed your welcome. From the bliss of a universe of free floating warm love you are thrust wriggling and writhing, cold and naked into the arms of a masked being surrounded by bright light who then throws you on to the stomach of your creator who, from your limited perspective, has to your horror turned inside out! No wonder the drink, the pill, the poem, the poet, the lost souls gathering dust on a shelf in a coffee shop in the City that Care Forgot.
